VANDA VANÍČKOVÁ

Simple Czech

Learn to Speak Czech for all Ages

HEALTHY LIVING

Contents

A Note From The Author

This book was created for visual learners to go hand in hand with the audiobook that is available on Audible and iTunes. It is highly recommended that this book is used as an aide to see the letters and words as you follow along with the audiobook. Listening to the audiobook will ensure that you really learn how to say and pronounce the Czech words from a real native Czech speaker like me!

Welcome! / Vítejte!

Welcome to Simple Czech; Learn to Speak Czech for All Ages! I am very excited that you want to learn Čeština [chesh-tina]. I am not going to lie to you. Czech can be very hard! That's why I have tried my best to make it simple for you. I have designed the lessons to be simple and fun for all ages.

- They are perfect for bilingual families just like mine! I know how it feels to be the only Czech speaking person in a family with an English-speaking partner and children.
- They are perfect for small children that are just starting to learn English and you would like them to learn Czech at the same time.
- They are also perfect for that partner that needs to start learning but doesn't quite know where to begin and how to approach it.
- You can practice in your car, on road trips, or going out for walks in nature.
- You can learn Simple Czech anywhere you are!

Through this book, I will be saying words in English, which is Angličtina, and we will have lots of fun learning how to speak and spell the words in Czech. I hope you're as excited as I am because very soon you will know the Czech alphabet and you will understand many words in the following categories:

- Basic words
- Days of the week
- Months and seasons
- Numbers
- And Family Members

If you love this book once you have completed all the lessons, I urge you to keep learning from the rest of the series that will be coming soon. We will have much more fun learning together in the future!

It would also mean so much to me if you could leave a review on Audible, Amazon, or iTunes to share your thoughts. When my book helps you or your child to learn the Czech language, then sharing a review is the best way to ensure that your feedback will help others like you find, and love, this book as much as you do. And now, the time has come to start your learning adventure!

Lesson 1: The Alphabet (Abeceda)

A B C Č D Ď
E Ě F G H CH
I J K L M N Ň
O P Q R Ř S
Š T Ť U V W
X Y Z Ž

We are going to start with the basics by learning all 35 letters in the Czech alphabet and how to say them! We are also going to learn how special characters, such as accent marks and hooks, can change the sounds of the vowels.

If you are more of a visual learner, I have a gift just for you! I have created a Simple Czech Supplement that has the entire alphabet and all the words that you will learn in this book so you can follow along. I am giving it to you completely **FREE!**

All you have to do is go to www.simpleczech.net and enter your email address on the form so that I will know where to send it to you. Let's begin the alphabet now! In Czech, the alphabet is called "Abeceda"

[Abets-eda]. Can you say Abeceda? Great job! Let's begin.

- The first letter of the alphabet is A. In Czech, this is A [ah]. A [ah]. A [ah]. Ok, why don't you say A [ah]. This is a great start, but let's say that one more time. A [ah]. I am sure you were able to say A [ah]. Awesome Job!

- The next letter is also an A, but it has an accent mark, or flag, over it. This makes a longer sound. Instead of A [ah], this is Á [ahh]. Á [ahh]. Ok, why don't you say Á [ahh]. Let's say that one more time. Á [ahh]. I am sure you can say Á [ahh]. Awesome Job!

- The next letter is B. In Czech, this is B [beh]. B [beh]. B [beh]. Ok, why don't you say B [beh]. Let's hear that one more time. B [beh]. I am sure you were able to say B [beh]. Great Job!

- The next letter is C. In Czech, this is C [tseh]. C [tseh]. C [tseh]. Ok, why don't you say C [tseh]. Can you say that one more time? C [tseh]. Were you able to say C [tseh]? Super Job!

- The next letter is also a C, but it has a hook over it. This makes a C-H sound. Instead of C [tseh], this is Č [cheh]. Č [cheh]. Č [cheh]. Ok, why don't you say Č [cheh]. Let's say that one more time. Č [cheh].

I am sure you can say Č [cheh]. Terrific Job!

- The next letter is D. In Czech, this is D [de]. D [de]. D [de]. Why don't you say D [de]. Let's hear that one more time. D [de]. I am sure you were able to say D [de]. Great Job!

- The next letter is also a D, but it has a hook over it. This makes a softer sound. Instead of D [de], this is Ď [dy'eh]. Ď [dy'eh]. Ď [dy'eh]. Ok, why don't you say Ď [dy'eh]. Let's say that one more time. Ď [dy'eh]. Were you able to say Ď [dy'eh]. Fantastic Job!

- The next letter is E. In Czech, this is E [eh]. E [eh]. Why don't you say E [eh]. Let's hear that one more time. E [eh]. I know you can say E [eh]. Great Job! You will see this vowel with both a flag over it and with a hook over it. When E[eh] has a flag over it, it makes a longer sound like É [ehh]. É [ehh]. Can you say É [ehh]? When E [eh] has a hook over it, it makes a softer sound like Ě [y'eah]. Ě [y'eah]. Ě [y'eah]. Can you say Ě [y'eah]? I knew you could!

- The next letter is F. In Czech, this is F [ef]. F [ef]. F [ef]. Why don't you say F [ef]. Let's hear that one more time. F [ef]. I am sure you were able to say F [ef]. Great Job!

- The next letter is G. In Czech, this is G [ge]. G [ge]. G [ge]. Why don't you say G [ge]. Let's hear that one more time. G [ge]. Were able to say G [ge]? Awesome Job!

- The next letter is H. In Czech, this is H [huh]. H [huh]. H [huh]. Why don't you say H [huh]. Let's say that again. H [huh]. Were able to say H [huh]? Fantastic Job!

- The next letter is a Ch together. Together they form one letter and they do not make the same sound as they do in English. In Czech, this letter is called Ch [Hhuh]. Ch [Hhuh]. Ch [Hhuh]. Why don't you try? Ch [Hhuh]. Let's say that one more time. Ch [Hhuh]. Can you say Ch [Hhuh]? Terrific Job!

- The next letter is I. In Czech, this is I [ee]. I [ee]. Why don't you say I [ee]. Let's hear that one more time. I [ee]. I know you can say I [ee]. Great Job! You will also see this vowel with a flag over it. When I [ee] has a flag over it, it makes a longer sound. It is called Í [eee]. Í [eee]. Can you say Í [eee]? I knew you could do it!

- The next letter is J. In Czech, this is J [yuh]. J [yuh]. J [yuh]. Why don't you say J [yuh]. Let's say that again. J [yuh]. Were able to say J [yuh]? Super Job!

- The next letter is K. In Czech, this is K [ka]. K [ka]. K [ka]. Why don't you say K [ka]. Let's say that again. K [ka]. Were able to say K [ka]? Great Job!

- The next letter is L. In Czech, this is the same as in English. It is L [el]. L [el]. I am pretty sure you are able to say L [el]. Great Job!

- The next letter is M. In Czech, this is also the same as in English. M [em]. M [em]. I am pretty sure you can say M [em]. Awesome!

- The next letter is N. In Czech, this is again the same as in English. It is N [en]. N [en]. I think you are able to say N [en]. Super Job!

- The next letter is also N, but it has a hook over it. This makes a softer sound. Instead of N [en], this letter is called Ň [en'eh]. Ň [en'eh]. Ň [en'eh]. Ok, why don't you say Ň [en'eh]. Let's try that one more time. Ň [en'eh]. Were you able to say Ň [en'eh]. Fantastic Job!

- The next letter is O. In Czech, this is O [o]. O [o]. Why don't you say O [o]. Let's hear that one more time. O [o]. I know you can say O [o]. Great Job! You will also see this vowel with a flag over it. When O

[o] has a flag over it, it makes a longer sound. It is called Ó [ooh]. Ó [ooh]. Can you say Ó [ooh]? I knew you could do it!

- The next letter is P. In Czech, this is P [pe]. P [pe]. P [pe]. Why don't you say P [pe]. Let's say that again. P [pe]. Were able to say P [pe]? Super Job!

- The next letter is Q. In Czech, this is Q [que]. Q [que]. Q [que]. Why don't you say Q [que]. Let's say that again. Q [que]. Were able to say Q [que]? Terrific!

- The next letter is R. In Czech, this is R [er]. R [er]. R [er]. Why don't you say R [er]. Why don't you say that again. R [er]. Were able to say R [er]? Perfect job!

- The next letter is also R, but it has a hook over it. This makes a tongue rolling sound. Instead of R [er], this letter is called Ř [e'dge]. Ř [e'dge]. Ř [e'dge]. Ok, why don't you say Ř [e'dge]. Let's try that one more time. Ř [e'dge]. Were you able to say Ř [e'dge]. Fantastic Job!

- The next letter is S. In Czech, this is the same as in English. It is S [es]. S [es]. I am pretty sure you are able to say S [es]. Great Job!

- The next letter is also S, but it has a hook over it. This makes an SH sound when used in words. Instead of S [es], this letter is called Š [esh]. Š [esh]. Š [esh]. Ok, why don't you say Š [esh]. Let's try that one more time. Š [esh]. Were you able to say Š [esh]. Super Job!

- The next letter is T. In Czech, this is T [te]. T [te]. T [te]. I am pretty sure you are able to say T [te]. Great Job!

- The next letter is also T, but it has a hook over it. This makes a softer sound. Instead of T [te], this letter is called Ť [ty'eh]. Ť [ty'eh]. Ť [ty'eh]. Ok, why don't you say Ť [ty'eh]. Let's try that one more time. Ť [ty'eh]. Were you able to say Ť [ty'eh]. Fantastic Job!

- The next letter is U. In Czech, this is U [ou]. U [ou]. Why don't you say U [ou]. Let's hear that one more time. U [ou]. I know you can say U [ou]. Great Job! You will see this vowel with both a flag over it and with a little circle over it. They both make a longer sound, and it's called Ú/Ů [ouu]. Ú/Ů [ouu]. Can you say Ú/Ů [ouu]? I knew you could!

- The next letter is V. In Czech, this is V [ve]. V [ve]. V [ve]. I am pretty sure you are able to say V [ve]. Great Job!

- The next letter is W. In Czech, this is W [di'voyte ve]. W [di'voyte ve]. W [di'voyte ve]. Ok, why don't you say W [di'voyte ve]. Let's try that one more time. W [di'voyte ve]. Were you able to say W [di'voyte ve]. Amazing Job!

- The next letter is X. In Czech, this is the same as in English. It is X [ex]. X [ex]. I am pretty sure you are able to say X [ex]. Great Job!

- The next letter is Y. In Czech, Y makes the same sound in words as it does in English such as in baby. The letter has an interesting name, however. It is called Y [ipsilone]. Y [ipsilone]. Y [ipsilone]. Why don't you say Y [ipsilone]. Let's hear that one more time. Y [ipsilone]. I know you can say Y [ipsilone]. Great Job! You will also see Y [ipsilone] with a flag over it. When Y [ipsilone] has a flag over it, it makes a longer sound. It is still called Ý [ipsilone]. Let's say it one more time. Ý [ipsilone]. I knew you could do it!

- The next letter is Z. In Czech, this is Z [zet]. Z [zet]. Z [zet]. I am pretty sure you are able to say Z [zet]. Excellent Job!

- The last letter is also Z, but it has a hook over it. Instead of Z [zet], this letter is called Ž [djet]. Ž [djet]. Ž [djet]. Ok, why don't you say Ž [djet]. Let's try that one more time. Ž [djet]. Were you able to say Ž [djet]. Awesome!

Fabulous job! You just learned the Czech alphabet, which does consist of some tricky new letters you have never seen before, and you know what? You nailed it! You should be proud of yourself. Learning the Czech alphabet, and being able to pronounce their unique sounds, is the first step to understanding the Czech language. Now we will review some Czech words and see if you can identify which letter each word begins with.

- The first word is Garáž. Garáž. In English, this is also Garage. Are you able to say "Garáž"? Awesome Job! Can you say the first letter of the word? The correct answer is G [ge]. The letter in English is G.

- The next word is Dům. Dům. In English, this is House. Are you able to say Dům? Great Job! I bet you know the first letter of the word. The correct answer is D [de]. The letter in English is D.

- The next word is Knížka. Knížka. In English, this means Little Book. Are you able to say Knížka? Super Job! Can you guess the first letter of the word? The correct answer is K [ka]. The letter in English is K.

- The next word is Taška. Taška. In English, this means Bag. Are you able to say Taška? Perfect! I am pretty sure you know the first letter of the word. You guessed it. It is T [te]. The letter in English is T.

- The next word is Sešit. Sešit. In English, this means Notebook. Are you able to say Sešit? Fantastic! I am pretty sure you know the first letter of the word. If you said S [es], you are correct again. The letter in English is S.

- The next word is Cirkus. Cirkus. In English, I am guessing you figured it out that this means Circus. Are you able to say Cirkus? Fantastic! I am pretty sure you know the first letter of the word too. The correct answer is C [tseh]. The letter in English is C.

· The next word is Opice. Opice. In English, this means Monkey. Are you able to say Opice? Great job! I am pretty sure you know the first letter of the word.The correct answer is O [o]. The letter in English is O.

· The next word is Ryba. Ryba. In English, this means Fish. Are you able to say Ryba? Awesome job! I bet you know the first letter of the word. The correct answer is R [er]. The letter in English is R.

· The next word is Zajíc. Zajíc. In English, this means Rabbit. Are you able to say Zajíc? Fabulous job! Do you know the first letter of the word? The correct answer is Z [zet]. The letter in English is Z.

- The next word is Ďábel. Ďábel. In English, this means Devil. Are you able to say Ďábel? Super Job! Can you guess the first letter of the word? The correct answer is Ď [dy'eh]. The letter in English is D with a hook.

- The next word is Nůžky. Nůžky. In English, this means Scissors. Are you able to say Nůžky? Perfect! I am pretty sure you know the first letter of the word. You guessed it. It is N [en]. The letter in English is N.

- The next word is Vítěz. Vítěz. In English, this means Winner. Are you able to say Vítěz? Fantastic! I am sure you know the first letter of the word. If you said V [ve], you are correct again. The letter in English is V.

- The next word is Fotky. Fotky. In English, this means Photos. Are you able to say Fotky? Great job! I am pretty sure you know the first letter of the word. The correct answer is F [ef]. The letter in English is also F.

- The next word is Chobotnice. Chobotnice. In English, this means Octopus. Are you able to say Chobotnice? Awesome job! Do you know the first letter of the word? It may not be what you think! The

16

correct answer is Ch [Hhuh]. The letter in English is Ch together. Ch [Hhuh].

· The next word is Lavice. Lavice. In English, this means Bench. Are you able to say Lavice? Fabulous job! I am sure you know the first letter of this word. That is right, it is L [el]. The letter in English is also L.

- The next word is Xylofon. Xylofon. In English, this means Xylophone. Are you able to say Xylofon? Super Job! Can you guess the first letter of the word? The correct answer is X [ex]. The letter in English is X also. Simple isn't it!

- The next word is Brýle. Brýle. In English, this means Reading Glasses. Are you able to say Brýle? Perfect! I am pretty sure you know the first letter of the word. You guessed it. It is B [beh]. The letter in English is B.

- The next word is Jablko. Jablko. In English, this means Apple. Are you able to say Jablko? Fantastic! Do you know the first letter of the word? If you said J [yuh], you are correct again. The letter in English is J.

- The next word is Eskymák. Eskymák. In English, this means Eskimo. Are you able to say Eskymák? Great job! Can you guess the first letter of the word? The correct answer is E [eh]. In English this is E.

- The next word is Řeka. Řeka. In English, this means River. Are you able to say Řeka? Awesome job! Do you know the first letter of the word? It may not be what you think! The correct answer is Ř [e'dge]. The letter in English is R with a hook over it.

- The next word is Šnek. Šnek. In English, this means Snail. Are you able to say Šnek? Fabulous job! Do you know the first letter of this word? The correct letter is Š [esh]. Don't forget the letter in English is S with a hook.

- The next word is Motýl. Motýl. In English, this means Butterfly. I think you are able to say Motýl. Super Job! I think you can guess the first letter of the word as well. The correct answer is M [em]. The letter in English is M also. I told you it was simple didn't I!

• The next word is Žába. Žába. In English, this means Frog. Are you able to say Žába? Perfect! This one isn't as simple. Do you know the first letter of the word. The correct answer is Ž [djet]. The letter in English is Z with a hook over it.

• The next word is Hokej. Hokej. In English, this means Hockey. Are you able to say Hokej? Fantastic! Do you know the first letter of the word? If you say H [huh], you are correct again. The letter in English is H.

• The next word is Pastelka. Pastelka. In English, this means Crayon. Are you able to say Pastelka? Great job! Can you guess the first letter of the word? The correct answer is P [pe]. In English that is P.

• The next word is Učitel. Učitel. In English, this means Teacher. Are you able to say Učitel? Awesome job! Do you know the first letter of the word? It may not be what you think! The correct answer is U [ou]. The letter in English is U.

- The next word is pretty simple. It is Itálie. Itálie. In English, this means Italy. I think you are able to say Itálie. Super Job! I think you can guess the first letter of the word as well. The correct answer is I [ee]. The letter in English is I.

· The final word is perhaps the simple of them all! It is Aligátor. Aligátor. In English, this means....you guessed it... Alligator. I think you are able to say Aligátor. Super Job! I think you can guess the first letter of the word as well. The correct answer is A [ah]. The letter in English is A. I told you it was the most simple didn't I!

Awesome job! You are starting to identify the sounds of the more complicated letters in the Czech language, and you did great! We have reached the end of the first lesson. The rest of the lessons will be much more fun, I promise! In the next lesson, we will be learning some very basic and simple words to get you started with speaking Czech!

Lesson 2: Basic Words (Základní slova)

Welcome back, and I hope you enjoyed learning the alphabet in lesson 1. Today in lesson 2, we will learn some essential Czech words, and phrases, that you need to know. In Czech, "Basic Words" is "Základní slova." Let's begin!

- The first word is Ano. **A-N-O**. Ano. Are you able to say Ano? Let's practice spelling the word. **A-N-O**. Are you able to spell Ano? Fantastic! In English, this means Yes.

- The next word is Ne. **N-E**. Ne. Are you able to say Ne? Let's practice spelling the word. **N-E**. Are you able to spell Ne? Great Job! In English, this means No.

- The next word is Děkuji. **D-Ě-K-U-J-I**. Děkuji. Can you say Děkuji? Let's practice spelling the word. **D-Ě-K-U-J-I**. Are you able to spell Děkuji? Fabulous Job! In English, this means Thank You.

- The next word is Prosím. **P-R-O-S-Í-M**. Prosím. Can you say Prosím? Let's practice spelling the word. **P-R-O-S-Í-M**. Are you able to spell Prosím? Super Job! In English, this means Please.

- The next phrase is Nemáš zač. **N-E-M-Á-Š Z-A-Č**. Nemáš zač. Can you say Nemáš zač? Let's practice spelling the word. **N-E-M-Á-Š**

Z-A-Č. Are you able to spell Nemáš zač? Perfect! In English, this means You're Welcome.

- The next word is Ahoj. **A-H-O-J**. Ahoj. Are you able to say Ahoj? Let's practice spelling the word. **A-H-O-J**. Are you able to spell Ahoj? Fantastic! In English, this means both Hello and Goodbye.

- The next word is Dobrý. **D-O-B-R-Ý**. Dobrý. Are you able to say Dobrý? Let's practice spelling the word. **D-O-B-R-Ý**. Are you able to spell Dobrý? Fantastic! In English, this means Good.

- The next phrase is Dobré ráno. **D-O-B-R-É R-Á-N-O**. Dobré ráno. Are you able to say Dobré ráno? Let's practice spelling the word. **D-O-B-R-É R-Á-N-O**. Are you able to spell Dobré ráno? Great Job! In English, this means Good Morning.

- The next phrase is Dobrý den. **D-O-B-R-Ý D-E-N**. Dobrý den. Can you say Dobrý den? Let's practice spelling the word. **D-O-B-R-Ý D-E-N**. Are you able to spell Dobrý den? Fabulous Job! In English, this means Good Day.

- The next word is Dobrý večer. **D-O-B-R-Ý V-E-Č-E-R**. Dobrý večer. Can you say Dobrý večer? Let's practice spelling the word. **D-O-B-R-Ý V-E-Č-E-R**. Are you able to spell Dobrý večer? Super Job! In English, this means Good Evening.

- The next phrase is Dobrou noc. **D-O-B-R-O-U N-O-C**. Dobrou noc. Can you say Dobrou noc? Let's practice spelling the word. **D-O-B-R-O-U N-O-C**. Are you able to spell Dobrou noc? Perfect! In English, this means Good Night.

- The next word is Na zdraví. **N-A Z-D-R-A-V-Í**. Na zdraví. Are you able to say Na zdraví? Let's practice spelling the word. **N-A Z-D-R-A-V-Í**. Are you able to spell Na zdraví? Fantastic! In English, this means both To Your Health or Cheers.

· The next phrase is Miluji tě. **M-I-L-U-J-I T-Ě**. Miluji tě. Are you able to say Miluji tě? Let's practice spelling the word. **M-I-L-U-J-I T-Ě**. Are you able to spell Miluji tě? Great Job! In English, this means I Love You.

- The next word is Kdo. **K-D-O**. Kdo. Can you say Kdo? Let's practice spelling the word. **K-D-O**. Are you able to spell Kdo? Fabulous Job! In English, this means Who.

- The next word is Co. **C-O**. Co. Can you say Co? Let's practice spelling the word. **C-O**. Are you able to spell Co? Super Job! In English, this means What.

- The next word is Když. **K-D-Y-Ž**. Když. Can you say Když? Let's practice spelling the word. **K-D-Y-Ž**. Are you able to spell Když? Perfect! In English, this means When.

- The next word is Kde. **K-D-E**. Kde. Are you able to say Kde? Let's practice spelling the word. **K-D-E**. Are you able to spell Kde? Fantastic! In English, this means Where.

- The next word is Proč. **P-R-O-Č**. Proč. Are you able to say Proč? Let's practice spelling the word. **P-R-O-Č**. Are you able to spell Proč? Great Job! In English, this means Why.

- The next word is Jak. **J-A-K**. Jak. Can you say Jak? Let's practice spelling the word. **J-A-K**. Are you able to spell Jak? Fabulous Job! In English, this means How.

- The next word is Protože. **P-R-O-T-O-Ž-E**. Protože. Can you say Protože? Let's practice spelling the word. **P-R-O-T-O-Ž-E**. Are you able to spell Protože? Super Job! In English, this means Because.

- The next word is Špatný. **Š-P-A-T-N-Ý**. Špatný. Can you say Špatný? Let's practice spelling the word. **Š-P-A-T-N-Ý**. Are you able to spell Špatný? Perfect! In English, this means Bad.

- The next word is To. **T-O**. To. Are you able to say To? Let's practice spelling the word. **T-O**. Are you able to spell To? Fantastic! In English, this means It.

- The next word is Je. **J-E**. Je. Are you able to say Je? Let's practice spelling the word. **J-E**. Are you able to spell Je? Great Job! In English, this means Is.

- The next word is Já. **J-Á**. Já. Can you say Já? Let's practice spelling the word. **J-Á**. Are you able to spell Já? Fabulous Job! In English, this means I, as in the sentence I love Simple Czech.

- The next word is Jsem. **J-S-E-M**. Jsem. Can you say Jsem? Let's practice spelling the word. **J-S-E-M**. Are you able to spell Jsem? Super Job! In English, this means I Am.

- The next word is Ty. **T-Y**. Ty. Can you say Ty? Let's practice spelling the word. **T-Y**. Are you able to spell Ty? Perfect! In English, this means You.

- The last phrase is Ty Jsi. **T-Y J-S-I**. Ty Jsi. Are you able to say Ty Jsi? Let's practice spelling the words. **T-Y J-S-I**. Are you able to spell Ty Jsi? Fantastic! In English, this means You Are.

Fantastic job! You just learned some basic Czech words that are important to know, and you did amazing! Now we will go over some of the Czech words and see if you can identify them and say what they mean in English.

- The first word is Prosím. **P-R-O-S-Í-M**. Prosím. Do you know what word that is in English? The correct answer is Please.

- The next word is Kde. **K-D-E**. Kde. Do you know what word that is in English? The correct answer is Where.

· The next phrase is Dobrou noc. **D-O-B-R-O-U N-O-C**. Dobrou noc. Do you know what that is in English? The correct answer is Good Night.

· The next phrase is Já. **J-Á**. Já. Do you know what that is in English? The correct answer is I.

· The next phrase is Dobré ráno. **D-O-B-R-É R-Á-N-O**. Dobré ráno. Do you know what that is in English? The correct answer is Good Morning.

· The next word is Ano. **A-N-O**. Ano. Do you know what word that is in English? The correct answer is Yes.

· The next word is Ahoj. **A-H-O-J**. Ahoj. Do you know what word that is in English? The correct answer is Hello or Goodbye.

- The next phrase is Miluji Tě. **M-I-L-U-J-I T-Ě**. Miluji Tě. Do you know what that is in English? The correct answer is I Love You.

- The next word is Proč. **P-R-O-Č**. Proč. Do you know what word that is in English? The correct answer is Why.

- The next word is Jsem. **J-S-E-M**. Jsem. Do you know what that is in English? The correct answer is I am.

- The next word is Špatný. **Š-P-A-T-N-Ý**. Špatný. Do you know what word that is in English? The correct answer is Bad.

- The next phrase is Dobrý den. **D-O-B-R-Ý D-E-N**. Dobrý den. Do you know what that is in English? The correct answer is Good Day.

- The next word is Ne. **N-E**. Ne. Do you know what word that is in English? The correct answer is No.

- The next phrase is Ty Jsi. **T-Y J-S-I**. Ty jsi. Do you know what that is in English? The correct answer is You are.

- The next word is Dobrý. **D-O-B-R-Ý**. Dobrý. Do you know what word that is in English? The correct answer is Good.

- The next word is Kdo. **K-D-O**. Kdo. Do you know what word that is in English? The correct answer is Who.

- The next word is Ty. **T-Y**. Ty. Do you know what word that is in English? The correct answer is You.

- The next word is Jak. **J-A-K**. Jak. Do you know what word that is in English? The correct answer is How.

- The next word is Co. **C-O**. Co. Do you know what word that is in English? The correct answer is What.

- The next word is Když. **K-D-Y-Ž**. Když. Do you know what word that is in English? The correct answer is When.

- The next word is Dobrý den. **D-O-B-R-Ý D-E-N**. Dobrý den. Do you know what word that is in English? The correct answer is Good Day.

- The next word is Děkuji. **D-Ě-K-U-J-I**. Děkuji. Do you know what word that is in English? The correct answer is Thank You.

- The next word is To. **T-O**. To. Do you know what word that is in English? The correct answer is It.

- The next word is Na zdraví. **N-A Z-D-R-A-V-Í**. Na zdraví. Do you know what word that is in English? The correct answer is both To Your Health or Cheers.

- The next word is Nemáš zač. **N-E-M-Á-Š Z-A-Č**. Nemáš zač. Do you know what word that is in English? The correct answer is You're Welcome.

- The next word is Je. **J-E**. Je. Do you know what word that is in English? If you think Is might be the correct answer, you would be correct.

- The next word is Protože. **P-R-O-T-O-Ž-E**. Protože. Do you know what word that is in English? The correct answer is Because.

- The last word is Dobrý večer. **D-O-B-R-Ý V-E-Č-E-R**. Dobrý večer. Do you know what word that is in English? The correct answer is Good Evening.

You did an incredible job! You are starting to learn the basic words that you need for conversations! This is exciting! We have come to the end of this lesson. In the next lesson, we will learn the days of the week in

Czech.

Lesson 3: Days of the Week (Dny v týdnu)

SUN   MON   TUE   WEN   THU   FRI   SAT

Ahoj kamaráde! That means Hello friend! Welcome to lesson 3, where we will review the week's days. In Czech, "Days of the Week" is "Dny v týdnu." Let's begin!

· The first word is Week. In Czech, this is Týden. **T-Ý-D-E-N**. Týden. Are you able to say Týden? Let's practice spelling the word. **T-Ý-D-E-N**. Are you able to spell Týden? Fantastic job!

· The next word is Monday. In Czech, this is Pondělí. **P-O-N-D-Ě-L-Í**. Pondělí. Can you say Pondělí? Let's practice spelling the word. **P-O-N-D-Ě-L-Í**. Can you spell Pondělí? Great Job!

- The next word is Tuesday. In Czech, this is Úterý. **Ú-T-E-R-Ý**. Úterý. Are you able to say Úterý? Let's practice spelling the word. **Ú-T-E-R-Ý**. Are you able to spell Úterý? Fabulous Job!

- The next word is Wednesday. In Czech, this is Středa. **S-T-Ř-E-D-A**. Středa. Can you say Středa? Let's practice spelling the word. **S-T-Ř-E-D-A**. Can you spell Středa? Super Job!

- The next word is Thursday. In Czech, this is Čtvrtek. **Č-T-V-R-T-E-K**. Čtvrtek. Are you able to say Čtvrtek? Let's practice spelling the word. **Č-T-V-R-T-E-K**. Are you able to spell Čtvrtek? Perfect!

- The next word is Friday. In Czech, this is Patek. **P-Á-T-E-K**. Pátek. Can you say Pátek? Let's practice spelling the word. **P-Á-T-E-K**. Can you spell Pátek? Fantastic job!

- The next word is Saturday. In Czech, this is Sobota. **S-O-B-O-T-A**. Sobota. Are you able to say Sobota? Let's practice spelling the word. **S-O-B-O-T-A**. Are you able to spell Sobota? Great job!

- The next word is Sunday. In Czech, this is Neděle. **N-E-D-É-L-E**. Neděle. Can you say Neděle? Let's practice spelling the word. **N-E-D-É-L-E**. Can you spell Neděle? Fabulous job!

Fantastic job! You just learned the days of the week in Czech, and you did great! Now we will go over the days of the week again, and we will see if you can identify them and say what they mean in English.

- The first word is Patek. **P-Á-T-E-K**. Patek. What do you think the word is in English? The correct answer is Friday.

- The next word is Úterý. **Ú-T-E-R-Ý**. Úterý. Do you know what word that is in English? If you said Tuesday, you are correct.

- The next word is Týden. **T-Ý-D-E-N**. Týden. What do you think the word is in English? The correct answer is Week.

- The next word is Sobota. **S-O-B-O-T-A**. Sobota. Do you know what word that is in English? If you said Saturday, you are correct.

- The next word is Čtvrtek. **Č-T-V-R-T-E-K**. Čtvrtek. What do you think the word is in English? The correct answer is Thursday.

- The next word is Pondělí. **P-O-N-D-Ě-L-Í**. Pondělí. Do you know what word that is in English? If you said Monday, you are correct.

- The next word is Středa. **S-T-Ř-E-D-A**. Středa. What do you think the word is in English? The correct answer is Wednesday.

- The next word is Neděle. **N-E-D-É-L-E**. Neděle. Do you know what word that is in English? If you said Sunday, you are correct.

You did great! You just learned the days of the week in Czech, and you were able to identify them and translate what they were in English! This is the end of this lesson. In the next lesson, we will learn Czech's months and seasons.

Lesson 4: Months and Seasons (Měsíce a roční období)

JANUARY   FEBRUARY   MARCH   APRIL

MAY   JUNE   JULY   AUGUST

SEPTEMBER   OCTOBER   NOVEMBER   DECEMBER

Welcome to lesson 4, where we will review the year's months and seasons. In Czech, "Months and Seasons" is "Měsíce a roční období." Let's begin!

- The first word is January. In Czech, this is Leden. **L-E-D-E-N**. Leden. Are you able to say Leden? Let's practice spelling the word. **L-E-D-E-N**. Are you able to spell Leden? Fantastic job!

- The next word is February. In Czech, this is Únor. **Ú-N-O-R**. Únor. Can you say Únor? Let's practice spelling the word. **Ú-N-O-R**. Can you spell Únor? Great Job!

- The next word is March. In Czech, this is Březen. **B-Ř-E-Z-E-N**. Březen. Are you able to say Březen? Let's practice spelling the word. **B-Ř-E-Z-E-N**. Are you able to spell Březen? Fabulous Job!

- The next word is April. In Czech, this is Duben. **D-U-B-E-N**. Duben. Can you say Duben? Let's practice spelling the word. **D-U-B-E-N**. Can you spell Duben? Super Job!

- The next word is May. In Czech, this is Květen. **K-V-Ě-T-E-N**. Květen. Are you able to say Květen? Let's practice spelling the word. **K-V-Ě-T-E-N**. Are you able to spell Květen? Perfect!

- The next word is June. In Czech, this is Červen. **Č-E-R-V-E-N**.

Červen. Can you say Červen? Let's practice spelling the word. **Č-E-R-V-E-N**. Can you spell Červen? Fantastic job!

- The next word is July. In Czech, this is Červenec. **Č-E-R-V-E-N-E-C**. Červenec. Are you able to say Červenec? Let's practice spelling the word. **Č-E-R-V-E-N-E-C**. Are you able to spell Červenec? Great job!

- The next word is August. In Czech, this is Srpen. **S-R-P-E-N**. Srpen. Can you say Srpen? Let's practice spelling the word. **S-R-P-E-N**. Can you spell Srpen? Fabulous job!

- The next word is September. In Czech, this is Září. **Z-Á-Ř-Í**. Září. Can you say Září? Let's practice spelling the word. **Z-Á-Ř-Í**. Can you spell Září? Super Job!

- The next word is October. In Czech, this is Říjen. **Ř-Í-J-E-N**. Říjen. Are you able to say Říjen? Let's practice spelling the word. **Ř-Í-J-E-N**. Are you able to spell Říjen? Perfect!

- The next word is November. In Czech, this is Listopad. **L-I-S-T-O-**

P-A-D. Listopad. Can you say Listopad? Let's practice spelling the word. **L-I-S-T-O-P-A-D.** Can you spell Listopad? Fantastic job!

· The next word is December. In Czech, this is Prosinec. **P-R-O-S-I-N-E-C.** Prosinec. Are you able to say Prosinec? Let's practice spelling the word. **P-R-O-S-I-N-E-C.** Are you able to spell Prosinec? Great job!

· The next word is Month. In Czech, this is Měsíc. **M-Ě-S-Í-C.** Měsíc. Can you say Měsíc? Let's practice spelling the word. **M-Ě-S-Í-C.** Can you spell Měsíc? Fabulous job!

· The next word is Year. In Czech, this is Rok. **R-O-K.** Rok. Can you say Rok? Let's practice spelling the word. **R-O-K.** Can you spell Rok? Super Job!

· The next word is Season. In Czech, this is Roční období. **R-O-Č-N-Í O-B-D-O-B-Í.** Roční období. Are you able to say Roční období? Let's practice spelling the word. **R-O-Č-N-Í O-B-D-O-B-Í.** Are you able to spell Roční období? Perfect!

45

- The next word is Spring. In Czech, this is Jaro. **J-A-R-O**. Jaro. Can you say Jaro? Let's practice spelling the word. **J-A-R-O**. Can you spell Jaro? Fantastic job!

- The next word is Summer. In Czech, this is Léto. **L-É-T-O**. Léto. Are you able to say Léto? Let's practice spelling the word. **L-É-T-O**. Are you able to spell Léto? Great job!

- The next word is Fall. In Czech, this is Podzim. **P-O-D-Z-I-M**. Podzim. Can you say Podzim? Let's practice spelling the word. **P-O-D-Z-I-M**. Can you spell Podzim? Fabulous job!

- The last word is Winter. In Czech, this is Zima. **Z-I-M-A**. Zima. Can you say Zima? Let's practice spelling the word. **Z-I-M-A**. Can you spell Zima? Super Job!

Perfect Job! You just learned the months and seasons in Czech, and you did awesome! I am super impressed with how much you're learning! Now we will go over the months and seasons again and see if you can identify them and say what they mean in English.

· The first word is Červenec. **Č-E-R-V-E-N-E-C**. Červenec. What do you think the word is in English? If you said July, you are correct.

· The next word is Rok. **R-O-K**. Rok. Do you know what word that is in English? The correct answer is Year.

- The next word is Duben. **D-U-B-E-N**. Duben. What do you think the word is in English? If you said April, you are correct.

- The next word is Listopad. **L-I-S-T-O-P-A-D**. Listopad. Do you know what word that is in English? The correct answer is November.

- The next word is Léto. **L-É-T-O**. Léto. What do you think the word is in English? If you said Summer, you are correct.

- The next word is Leden. **L-E-D-E-N**. Leden. Do you know what word that is in English? The correct answer is January.

- The next word is Září. **Z-Á-Ř-Í**. Září. What do you think the word is in English? If you said September, you are correct.

- The next word is Měsíc. **M-Ě-S-Í-C**. Měsíc. Do you know what word that is in English? The correct answer is Month.

- The first word is Zima. **Z-I-M-A**. Zima. What do you think the word is in English? The correct answer is Winter.

- The next word is Únor. **Ú-N-O-R**. Únor. Do you know what word that is in English? If you said February, you are correct.

- The next word is Roční období. **R-O-Č-N-Í O-B-D-O-B-Í**. Roční období. What do you think the word is in English? The correct answer is Season.

- The next word is Květen. **K-V-Ě-T-E-N**. Květen. Do you know what word that is in English? If you said May, you are correct.

- The next word is Srpen. **S-R-P-E-N**. Srpen. What do you think the word is in English? The correct answer is August.

- The next word is Prosinec. **P-R-O-S-I-N-E-C**. Prosinec. Do you know what word that is in English? If you said December, you are correct.

- The next word is Jaro. **J-A-R-O**. Jaro. What do you think the word is in English? The correct answer is Spring.

- The next word is Březen. **B-Ř-E-Z-E-N**. Březen. Do you know what word that is in English? If you said March, you are correct.

- The next word is Červen. **Č-E-R-V-E-N**. Červen. What do you think the word is in English? The correct answer is June.

- The next word is Říjen. **Ř-Í-J-E-N**. Říjen. Do you know what word that is in English? If you said October, you are correct.

- The last word is Podzim. **P-O-D-Z-I-M**. Podzim. What do you think the word is in English? The correct answer is Fall.

You did so good! You just learned the months and seasons in Czech, and you could identify them and translate them into English! This lesson has come to an end. In the next lesson, we will get back to it and be learning numbers in Czech.

Lesson 5: Numbers (Čísla)

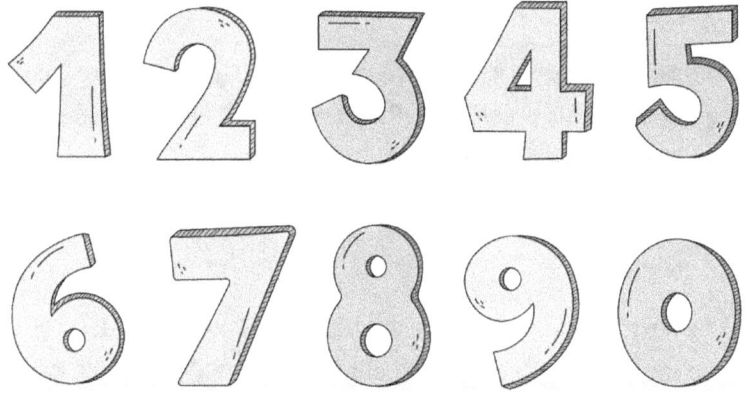

Welcome back! Today in lesson 5, we will be going over numbers in Czech. In Czech, "Numbers" is "Čísla." Let's begin!

- The first number is 0. In Czech, this is Nula. **N-U-L-A**. Nula. Are you able to say Nula? Let's practice spelling the word. **N-U-L-A**. Are you able to spell Nula? Fantastic job!

- The next number is 1. In Czech, this is Jedna. **J-E-D-N-A**. Jedna. Are you able to say Jedna? Let's practice spelling the word. **J-E-D-N-A**. Are you able to spell Jedna? Fantastic job!

- The next number is 2. In Czech, this is Dva. **D-V-A**. Dva. Can you say Dva? Let's practice spelling the word. D-V-A. Can you spell Dva? Great Job!

- The next number is 3. In Czech, this is Tři. **T-Ř-I**. Tři. Are you able to say Tři? Let's practice spelling the word. **T-Ř-I**. Are you able to spell Tři? Fabulous Job!

- The next number is 4. In Czech, this is Čtyři. **Č-T-Y-Ř-I**. Čtyři. Can you say Čtyři? Let's practice spelling the word. **Č-T-Y-Ř-I**. Can you spell Čtyři? Super Job!

- The next number is 5. In Czech, this is Pět. **P-Ě-T**. Pět. Are you able to say Pět? Let's practice spelling the word. **P-Ě-T**. Are you able to spell Pět? Perfect!

- The next number is 6. In Czech, this is Šest. **Š-E-S-T**. Šest. Can you say Šest? Let's practice spelling the word. **Š-E-S-T**. Can you spell Šest? Fantastic job!

· The next number is 7. In Czech, this is Sedm. **S-E-D-M**. Sedm. Are you able to say Sedm? Let's practice spelling the word. **S-E-D-M**. Are you able to spell Sedm? Great job!

· The next number is 8. In Czech, this is Osm. **O-S-M**. Osm. Can you say Osm? Let's practice spelling the word. **O-S-M**. Can you spell Osm? Fabulous job!

· The next number is 9. In Czech, this is Devět. **D-E-V-Ě-T**. Devět. Can you say Devět? Let's practice spelling the word. **D-E-V-Ě-T**. Can you spell Devět? Super Job!

· The next number is 10. In Czech, this is Deset. **D-E-S-E-T**. Deset. Are you able to say Deset? Let's practice spelling the word. **D-E-S-E-T**. Are you able to spell Deset? Perfect!

· The next number is 11. In Czech, this is Jedenáct. **J-E-D-E-N-Á-C-T**. Jedenáct. Can you say Jedenáct? Let's practice spelling the word.

53

J-E-D-E-N-Á-C-T. Can you spell Jedenáct? Fantastic job!

· The next number is 12. In Czech, this is Dvanáct. **D-V-A-N-Á-C-T.** Dvanáct. Are you able to say Dvanáct? Let's practice spelling the word. **D-V-A-N-Á-C-T.** Are you able to spell Dvanáct? Great job!

· The next number is 13. In Czech, this is Třináct. **T-Ř-I-N-Á-C-T.** Třináct. Can you say Třináct? Let's practice spelling the word. **T-Ř-I-N-Á-C-T.** Can you spell Třináct? Fabulous job!

· The next number is 14. In Czech, this is Čtrnáct. **Č-T-R-N-Á-C-T.** Čtrnáct. Can you say Čtrnáct? Let's practice spelling the word. **Č-T-R-N-Á-C-T.** Can you spell Čtrnáct? Super Job!

· The next number is 15. In Czech, this is Patnáct. **P-A-T-N-Á-C-T.** Patnáct. Are you able to say Patnáct? Let's practice spelling the word. **P-A-T-N-Á-C-T.** Are you able to spell Patnáct? Perfect!

· The next number is 16. In Czech, this is Šestnáct. **Š-E-S-T-N-Á-C-T.** Šestnáct. Can you say Šestnáct? Let's practice spelling the word. **Š-E-S-T-N-Á-C-T.** Can you spell Šestnáct? Fantastic job!

- The next number is 17. In Czech, this is Sedmnáct. **S-E-D-M-N-Á-C-T**. Sedmnáct. Are you able to say Sedmnáct? Let's practice spelling the word. **S-E-D-M-N-Á-C-T**. Are you able to spell Sedmnáct? Great job!

- The next number is 18. In Czech, this is Osmnáct. **O-S-M-N-Á-C-T**. Osmnáct. Can you say Osmnáct? Let's practice spelling the word. **O-S-M-N-Á-C-T**. Can you spell Osmnáct? Fabulous job!

- The next number is 19. In Czech, this is Devatenáct. **D-E-V-A-T-E-N-Á-C-T**. Devatenáct. Can you say Devatenáct? Let's practice spelling the word. **D-E-V-A-T-E-N-Á-C-T**. Can you spell Devatenáct? Super Job!

- The next number is 20. In Czech, this is Dvacet. **D-V-A-C-E-T**. Dvacet. Can you say Dvacet? Let's practice spelling the word. **D-V-A-C-E-T**. Can you spell Dvacet? Fabulous job!

Now after twenty, it gets easier to remember the numbers. 21 is just Twenty and One together, Dvacet Jedna. 22 is Twenty and Two together Dvacet Dva. That continues until 29. Then it continues from 31 to 39 also. And then from 41 to 49. Therefore, we will focus on only 30, 40, 50, 60, 70, 80, 90, and 100.

- The next number is 30. In Czech, this is Třicet. **T-Ř-I-C-E-T**. Třicet. Can you say Třicet? Let's practice spelling the word. **T-Ř-I-C-E-T**. Can you spell Třicet? Fabulous job!

- The next number is 40. In Czech, this is Čtyřicet. **Č-T-Y-Ř-I-C-E-T**. Čtyřicet. Can you say Čtyřicet? Let's practice spelling the word. **Č-T-Y-Ř-I-C-E-T**. Can you spell Čtyřicet? Fabulous job!

- The next number is 50. In Czech, this is Padesát. **P-A-D-E-S-Á-T**. Padesát. Can you say Padesát? Let's practice spelling the word. **P-A-D-E-S-Á-T**. Can you spell Padesát? Fabulous job!

- The next number is 60. In Czech, this is Šedesát. **Š-E-D-E-S-Á-T**. Šedesát. Can you say Šedesát? Let's practice spelling the word. **Š-E-D-E-S-Á-T**. Can you spell Šedesát? Fabulous job!

- The next number is 70. In Czech, this is Sedmdesát. **S-E-D-M-D-E-S-Á-T**. Sedmdesát. Can you say Sedmdesát? Let's practice spelling the word. **S-E-D-M-D-E-S-Á-T**. Can you spell Sedmdesát? Fabulous job!

- The next number is 80. In Czech, this is Osmdesát. **O-S-M-D-E-S-Á-T**. Osmdesát. Can you say Osmdesát? Let's practice spelling the word. **O-S-M-D-E-S-Á-T**. Can you spell Osmdesát? Fabulous job!

- The next number is 90. In Czech, this is Devadesát. **D-E-V-A-D-E-S-Á-T**. Devadesát. Can you say Devadesát? Let's practice spelling the word. **D-E-V-A-D-E-S-Á-T**. Can you spell Devadesát? Fabulous job!

- The last number is 100. In Czech, this is Sto. **S-T-O**. Sto. Can you say Sto? Let's practice spelling the word. **S-T-O**. Can you spell Sto? Fabulous job!

Wow, that was a lot of numbers, but you did it! You just learned the numbers in Czech up to 100, and you did perfectly! Now we will go over the numbers again and see if you can identify them and say what they mean in English.

- The first number is Šest. **Š-E-S-T**. Šest. What do you think the number is in English? If you said 6, you are correct.

- The next number is Tři. **T-Ř-I**. Tři. Do you know what number that is in English? The correct answer is 3.

- The next number is Devět. **D-E-V-Ě-T**. Devět. What do you think the number is in English? If you said 9, you are correct.

- The next number is Dva. **D-V-A**. Dva. Do you know what number that is in English? The correct answer is 2.

- The next number is Pět. **P-Ě-T**. Pět. What do you think the number is in English? If you said 5, you are correct.

- The next number is Osm. **O-S-M**. Osm. Do you know what number that is in English? The correct answer is 8.

- The next number is Jedna. **J-E-D-N-A**. Jedna. What do you think the number is in English? If you said 1, you are correct.

- The next number is Čtyři. **Č-T-Y-Ř-I**. Čtyři. Do you know what number that is in English? The correct answer is 4.

- The next number is Sedm. **S-E-D-M**. Sedm. What do you think the number is in English? If you said 7, you are correct.

- The next number is Nula. **N-U-L-A**. Nula. What do you think the number is in English? If you said 0, you are correct.

- The next number is Deset. **D-E-S-E-T**. Deset. Do you know what number that is in English? The correct answer is 10.

- The next number is Patnáct. **P-A-T-N-Á-C-T**. Patnáct. What do you think the number is in English? If you said 15, you are correct.

- The next number is Osmnáct. **O-S-M-N-Á-C-T**. Osmnáct. Do you know what number that is in English? The correct answer is 18.

- The next number is Třináct. **T-Ř-I-N-Á-C-T**. Třináct. What do you think the number is in English? If you said 13, you are correct.

- The next number is Devatenáct. **D-E-V-A-T-E-N-Á-C-T**. Devatenáct. Do you know what number that is in English? The correct answer is 19.

- The next number is Jedenáct. **J-E-D-E-N-Á-C-T**. Jedenáct. What do you think the number is in English? If you said 11, you are correct.

- The next number is Šestnáct. **Š-E-S-T-N-Á-C-T**. Šestnáct. Do you know what number that is in English? The correct answer is 16.

- The next number is Dvanáct. **D-V-A-N-Á-C-T**. Dvanáct. What do you think the number is in English? If you said 12, you are correct.

- The next number is Sedmnáct. **S-E-D-M-N-Á-C-T**. Sedmnáct. Do you know what number that is in English? The correct answer is 17.

- The next number is Čtrnáct. **Č-T-R-N-Á-C-T**. Čtrnáct. What do you think the number is in English? If you said 14, you are correct.

- The next number is Dvacet. **D-V-A-C-E-T**. Dvacet. Do you know what number that is in English? The correct answer is 20.

- The next number is Šedesát. **Š-E-D-E-S-Á-T**. Šedesát. What do you think the number is in English? If you said 60, you are correct.

- The next number is Sto. **S-T-O**. Sto. Do you know what number that is in English? The correct answer is 100.

- The next number is Osmdesát. **O-S-M-D-E-S-Á-T**. Osmdesát. What do you think the number is in English? If you said 80, you are correct.

- The next number is Třicet. **T-Ř-I-C-E-T**. Třicet. Do you know what number that is in English? The correct answer is 30.

- The next number is Padesát. **P-A-D-E-S-Á-T**. Padesát. What do you think the number is in English? If you said 50, you are correct.

- The next number is Sedmdesát. **S-E-D-M-D-E-S-Á-T**. Sedmdesát. Do you know what number that is in English? The correct answer is 70.

- The next number is Čtyřicet. **Č-T-Y-Ř-I-C-E-T**. Čtyřicet. What do you think the number is in English? If you said 40, you are correct.

- The last number is Devadesát. **D-E-V-A-D-E-S-Á-T**. Devadesát. Do you know what number that is in English? The correct answer is 90.

You did amazing! You just learned the numbers in Czech up to 100, and you were able to identify them and translate what they were in English! This was the longest lesson, and you made it! You are well on your way to speaking more Czech!

Lesson 6: Family (Rodina)

Ahoj! I am so glad you are back. In this next lesson, we will be talking about the different people that may be in your family. In Czech, "Family" is "Rodina". Let's begin!

- The first word is Muž. **M-U-Ž**. Muž. Are you able to say Muž? Let's practice spelling the word. **M-U-Ž**. Are you able to spell Muž? Fantastic job! In English, this means Man.

- The next word is Žena. **Ž-E-N-A**. Žena. Are you able to say Žena? Let's practice spelling the word. **Ž-E-N-A**. Are you able to spell Žena? Great Job! In English, this means Woman.

- The next word is Chlapec. **CH-L-A-P-E-C**. Chlapec. Are you able to say Chlapec? Let's practice spelling the word. **CH-L-A-P-E-C**. Are you able to spell Chlapec? Fabulous Job! In English, this means Boy.

- The next word is Dívka. **D-Í-V-K-A**. Dívka. Are you able to say Dívka? Let's practice spelling the word. **D-Í-V-K-A**. Are you able to spell Dívka? Super Job! In English, this means Girl.

- The next word is Otec. **O-T-E-C**. Otec. Are you able to say Otec? Let's practice spelling the word. **O-T-E-C**. Are you able to spell Otec? Perfect! In English, this means Father.

- The next word is Táta. **T-Á-T-A**. Táta. Are you able to say Táta? Let's practice spelling the word. **T-Á-T-A**. Are you able to spell Táta? Fantastic job! In English, this means Dad.

- The next word is Matka. **M-A-T-K-A**. Matka. Are you able to say

Matka? Let's practice spelling the word. **M-A-T-K-A**. Are you able to spell Matka? Great Job! In English, this means Mother.

- The next word is Maminka. **M-A-M-I-N-K-A**. Maminka. Are you able to say Maminka? Let's practice spelling the word. **M-A-M-I-N-K-A**. Are you able to spell Maminka? Fabulous Job! In English, this means Mom.

- The next word is Bratr. **B-R-A-T-R**. Bratr. Are you able to say Bratr? Let's practice spelling the word. **B-R-A-T-R**. Are you able to spell Bratr? Super Job! In English, this means Brother.

- The next word is Sestra. **S-E-S-T-R-A**. Sestra. Are you able to say Sestra? Let's practice spelling the word. **S-E-S-T-R-A**. Are you able to spell Sestra? Perfect! In English, this means Sister.

- The next word is Dědeček. **D-Ě-D-E-Č-E-K**. Dědeček. Are you able to say Dědeček? Let's practice spelling the word. **D-Ě-D-E-Č-E-K**. Are you able to spell Dědeček? Fantastic job! In English, this means Grandfather.

- The next word is Babička. **B-A-B-I-Č-K-A**. Babička. Are you able to say Babička? Let's practice spelling the word. **B-A-B-I-Č-K-A**. Are you able to spell Babička? Great Job! In English, this means Grandmother.

- The next word is Strýc. **S-T-R-Ý-C**. Strýc. Are you able to say Strýc? Let's practice spelling the word. **S-T-R-Ý-C**. Are you able to spell Strýc? Fabulous Job! In English, this means Uncle.

- The next word is Teta. **T-E-T-A**. Teta. Are you able to say Teta? Let's practice spelling the word. **T-E-T-A**. Are you able to spell Teta? Super Job! In English, this means Aunt.

- The next word is Bratranec. **B-R-A-T-R-A-N-E-C**. Bratranec. Are you able to say Bratranec? Let's practice spelling the word. **B-R-A-T-R-A-N-E-C**. Are you able to spell Bratranec? Perfect! In English, this means Boy Cousin.

- The next word is Sestřenice. **S-E-S-T-Ř-E-N-I-C-E**. Sestřenice. Are you able to say Sestřenice? Let's practice spelling the word. **S-E-S-T-Ř-E-N-I-C-E**. Are you able to spell Sestřenice? Perfect! In English, this means Girl Cousin.

- The next word is Synovec. **S-Y-N-O-V-E-C**. Synovec. Are you able to say Synovec? Let's practice spelling the word. **S-Y-N-O-V-E-C**. Are you able to spell Synovec? Fantastic job! In English, this means Nephew.

- The next word is Neteř. **N-E-T-E-Ř**. Neteř. Are you able to say Neteř? Let's practice spelling the word. **N-E-T-E-Ř**. Are you able to spell Neteř? Great Job! In English, this means Niece.

- The next word is Tchán. **T-CH-Á-N**. Tchán. Are you able to say Tchán? Let's practice spelling the word. **T-CH-Á-N**. Are you able to spell Tchán? Fabulous Job! In English, this means Father-in-law.

- The next word is Tchyně. **T-CH-Y-N-Ě**. Tchyně. Are you able to say Tchyně? Let's practice spelling the word. **T-CH-Y-N-Ě**. Are you able to spell Tchyně? Super Job! In English, this means Mother-in-law.

- The next word is Švagr. **Š-V-A-G-R**. Švagr. Are you able to say Švagr? Let's practice spelling the word. **Š-V-A-G-R**. Are you able to spell Švagr? Perfect! In English, this means Brother-in-law.

- The last word is Švagrová. **Š-V-A-G-R-O-V-Á**. Švagrová. Are you able to say Švagrová? Let's practice spelling the word. **Š-V-A-G-R-O-V-Á**. Are you able to spell Švagrová? Fantastic job! In English, this means Sister-in-law.

Amazing! You just learned about the different people that may be in your family in Czech, and you did super! Now we will go over family again and see if you can identify them and say what they mean in English.

- The first word is Babička. **B-A-B-I-Č-K-A**. Babička. What do you think the word is in English? If you said Grandmother, you are correct.

- The next word is Táta. **T-Á-T-A**. Táta. Do you know what word that is in English? The correct answer is Dad.

- The next word is Tchán. **T-CH-Á-N**. Tchán. What do you think the word is in English? If you said Father-in-law, you are correct.

- The next word is Bratr. **B-R-A-T-R**. Bratr. Do you know what word that is in English? The correct answer is Brother.

- The next word is Chlapec. **CH-L-A-P-E-C**. Chlapec. What do you think the word is in English? If you said Boy, you are correct.

- The next word is Bratranec. **B-R-A-T-R-A-N-E-C**. Bratranec. Do you know what word that is in English? The correct answer is Boy Cousin.

- The next word is Švagr. **Š-V-A-G-R**. Švagr. What do you think the word is in English? If you said Brother-in-law, you are correct.

- The next word is Muž. **M-U-Ž**. Muž. Do you know what word that is in English? The correct answer is Man.

- The next word is Sestra. **S-E-S-T-R-A**. Sestra. What do you think the word is in English? If you said Sister, you are correct.

- The next word is Synovec. **S-Y-N-O-V-E-C**. Synovec. Do you know what word that is in English? The correct answer is Nephew.

- The next word is Švagrová. **Š-V-A-G-R-O-V-Á**. Švagrová. What do you think the word is in English? If you said Sister-in-law, you are correct.

- The next word is Otec. **O-T-E-C**. Otec. Do you know what word that is in English? The correct answer is Father.

- The next word is Teta. **T-E-T-A**. Teta. What do you think the word is in English? If you said Aunt, you are correct.

- The next word is Maminka. **M-A-M-I-N-K-A**. Maminka. Do you know what word that is in English? The correct answer is Mom.

- The next word is Dívka. **D-Í-V-K-A**. Dívka. What do you think the word is in English? If you said Girl, you are correct.

- The next word is Neteř. **N-E-T-E-Ř**. Neteř. Do you know what word that is in English? The correct answer is Niece.

- The next word is Žena. **Ž-E-N-A**. Žena. What do you think the word is in English? If you said Woman, you are correct.

- The next word is Dědeček. **D-Ě-D-E-Č-E-K**. Dědeček. Do you know what word that is in English? The correct answer is Grandfather.

- The next word is Tchyně. **T-CH-Y-N-Ě**. Tchyně. What do you think the word is in English? If you said Mother-in-law, you are correct.

- The next word is Strýc. **S-T-R-Ý-C**. Strýc. Do you know what word that is in English? The correct answer is Uncle.

- The next word is Matka. **M-A-T-K-A**. Matka. What do you think the word is in English? If you said Mother, you are correct.

- Last word is Sestřenice. **S-E-S-T-Ř-E-N-I-C-E**. Sestřenice. What do you think the word is in English? If you said Girl Cousin, you are correct.

You did tremendously! You just learned about the different people that may be in your family in Czech, and you were able to identify them and translate what they were in English! This is the end of the final lesson!!! Congratulations!!!

Congratulations! You Have Finished!

Nas chledanou kamaráde! This means goodbye friend! I hope you enjoyed learning Czech with me. Make sure to keep practicing your lessons, and mastering what you have learned with me. Thank you so much for listening to Simple Czech. If you enjoyed this audiobook, please leave a review on Audible, Amazon, or iTunes and share your thoughts with others. If you let other potential listeners know just how much you loved this audiobook, that can help them make an informed decision so they can love it too. Don't forget to visit www.simpleczech.net to get your free Simple Czech supplement.

I am also proud to announce that Simple Czech Volume 2 will be released later in 2024, so that you will able to continue your journey of learning the Czech language. In Simple Czech Volume 2 you will be learning:

· Transportation
· Things you wear
· Parts of the body
· Foods and drinks
· Fruits and vegetables
· And much more!!!!

About the Author

Native Czech speaker Vanda Vaníčková is the author of *Simple Czech*.

Her work is dedicated to teaching the Czech language in a fun way, designed for optimum retention and understanding.

Vanda was born in Czechoslovakia, the country now known as the Czech Republic. She moved to the United States in her early 20's, specifically to improve her English skills and learn about American culture. She had no idea at that time that she would build a life in the US, but when she met the man who would become her husband, she never looked back. 23 years later, she still lives in the States with her English-speaking husband and two daughters.

It was this family setup that inspired Vanda to write language books. She found herself constantly searching for simple tools to help her husband and children learn Czech so that they could communicate with her family. After extensive research and a long journey of figuring out what worked best for her whole family (regardless of their age), she wrote, published, and narrated *Simple Czech* in order to help other families pick up the language when their lives are already filled with other commitments.

Vanda is an entrepreneur with a background in chemistry. She lives with her husband and two children in North Carolina and takes every opportunity she can to teach them more about her home country and its language.

You can connect with me on:

🌐 https://simpleczech.net

www.ingramcontent.com/pod-product-compliance
Lightning Source LLC
Chambersburg PA
CBHW070448130626
46553CB00006B/2306